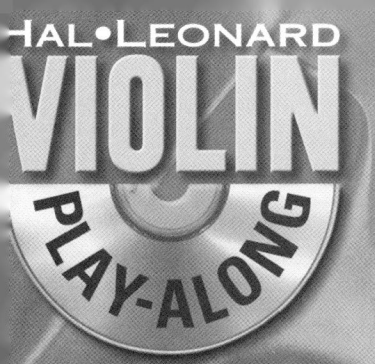

HAL•LEONARD VIOLIN PLAY-ALONG

Wedding Favorites

VOL. 13

CONTENTS

Page	Title	Demo Track	Play-Along Track
2	All I Ask of You	1	2
9	Highland Cathedral	3	4
4	In My Life	5	6
6	Somewhere Out There	7	8
10	Sunrise, Sunset	9	10
12	A Time for Us (Love Theme)	11	12
14	We've Only Just Begun	13	14
16	Wedding Processional	15	16
	TUNING NOTES	17	

ISBN 978-1-4234-6197-5

HAL•LEONARD CORPORATION
7777 W. BLUEMOUND RD. P.O. BOX 13819 MILWAUKEE, WI 53213

Recorded and Produced by Dan Maske
Gerald Loughney, Violin
Dan Maske, additional instruments

For all works contained herein:
Unauthorized copying, arranging, adapting,
recording, Internet posting, public performance,
or other distribution of the printed or recorded music
in this publication is an infringement of copyright.
Infringers are liable under the law.

Visit Hal Leonard Online at
www.halleonard.com

All I Ask of You

from THE PHANTOM OF THE OPERA

Music by ANDREW LLOYD WEBBER
Lyrics by CHARLES HART
Additional Lyrics by RICHARD STILGOE

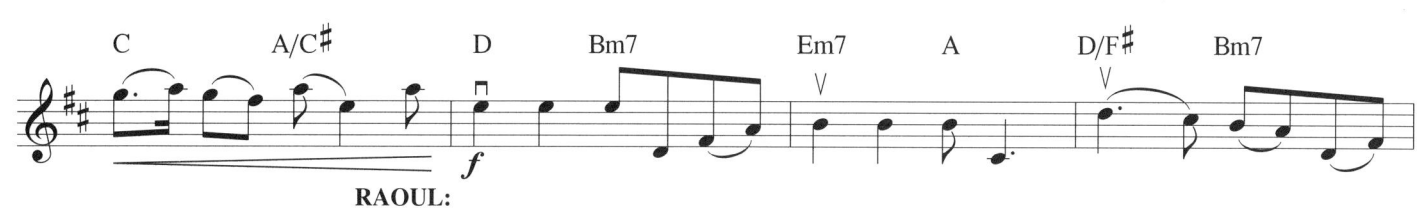

RAOUL: hold me and to hide me. Then say you'll share with me one love, one life-time; let me lead you from your sol-i-tude. Say you need me with you; here be-side you; an-y-where you go, let me go too. Chris-tine, that's all I ask of you.

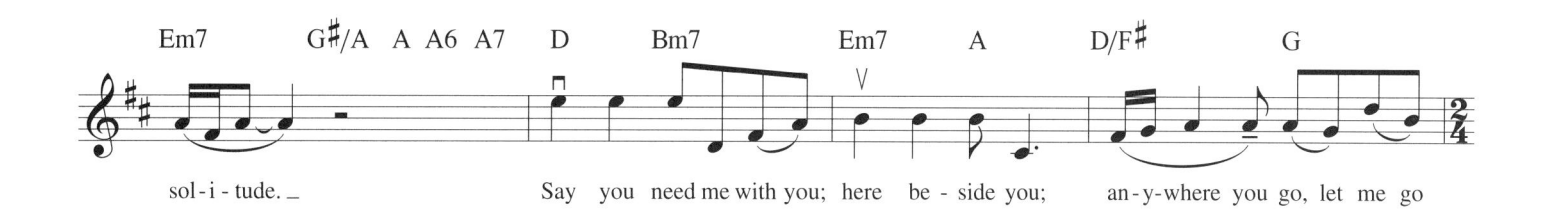

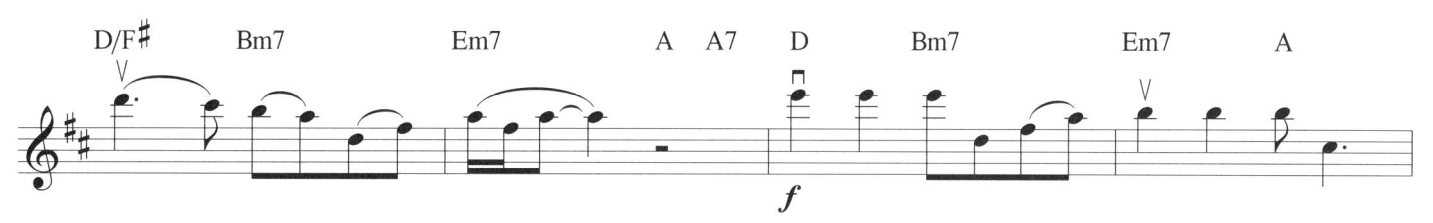

CHRISTINE: Say you'll share with me one love, one life-time; say the word and I will fol-low you. **TOGETHER:** Share each day with me, each night, each morn-ing.

CHRISTINE: Say you love me! **RAOUL & CHRISTINE:** Love me, that's all I ask of you.
RAOUL: You know I do.

CHRISTINE & RAOUL: An-y-where you go, let me go too; **RAOUL & CHRISTINE:** love me, that's all I ask of you.

In My Life

Words and Music by JOHN LENNON
and PAUL McCARTNEY

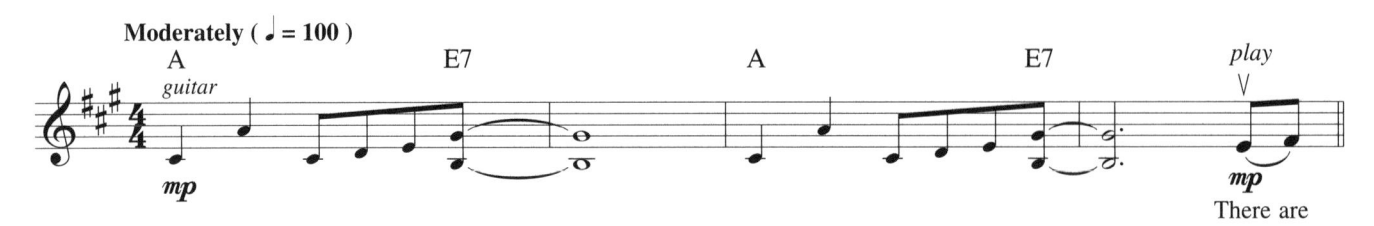

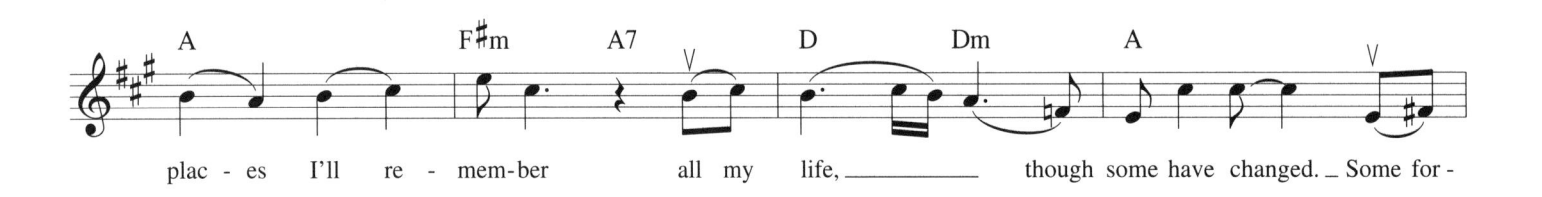

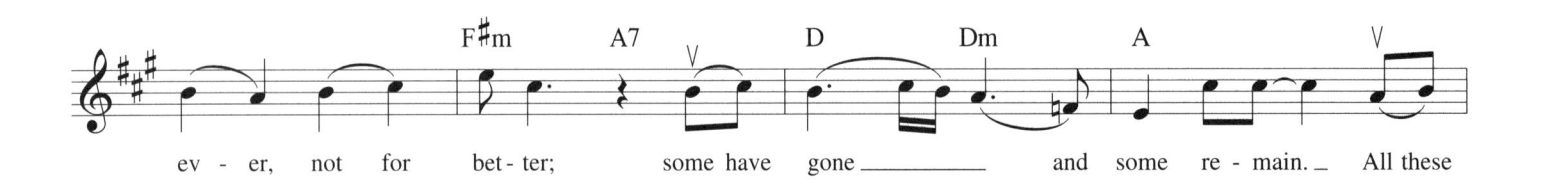

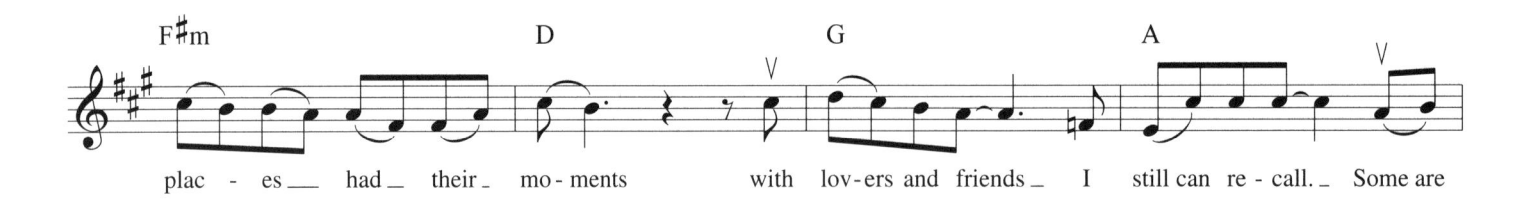

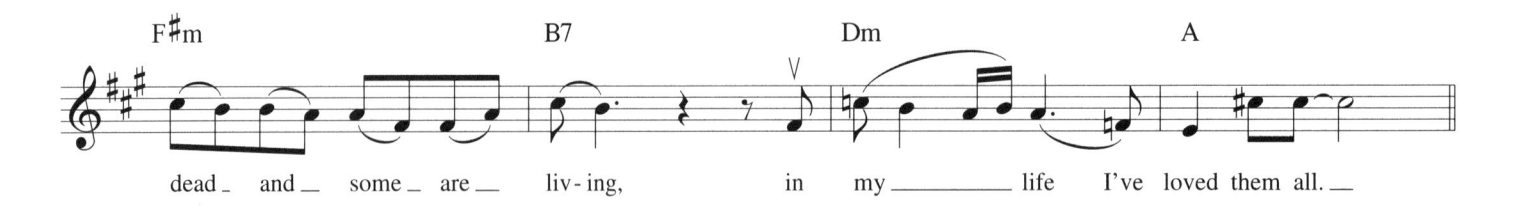

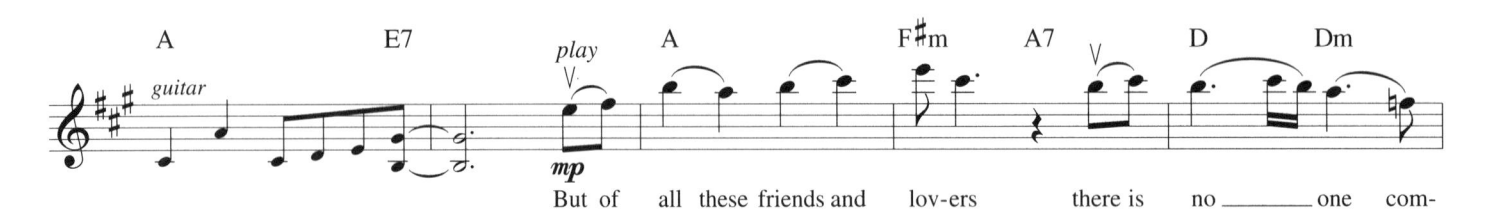

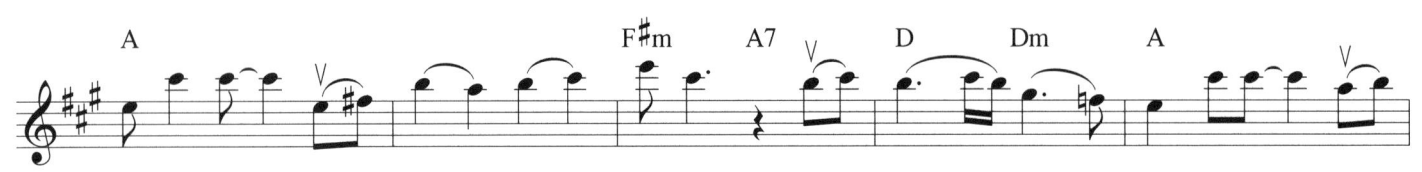

There are places I'll remember all my life, though some have changed. Some forever, not for better; some have gone and some remain. All these places had their moments with lovers and friends I still can recall. Some are dead and some are living, in my life I've loved them all. But of all these friends and lovers there is no one compares with you. And these mem'ries lose their meaning when I think of love as something new. Tho' I know I'll never lose affection for people and things that went before, I know I'll often stop and think about them, in my life I love you more.

Tho' I know I'll never lose affection for people and things that went before, I know I'll often stop and think about them, in my life I love you more.

In my life I love you more.

Somewhere Out There

from AN AMERICAN TAIL

Music by BARRY MANN and James Horner
Lyric by CYNTHIA WEIL

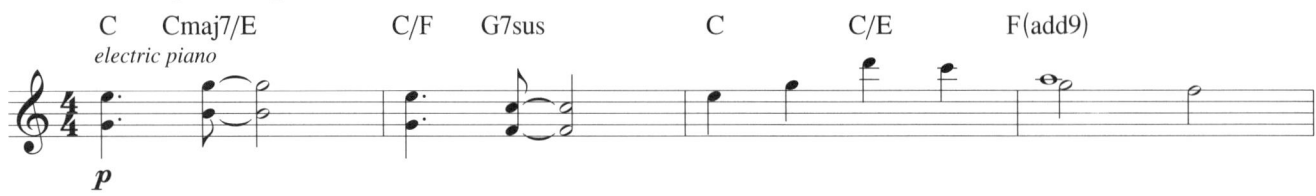

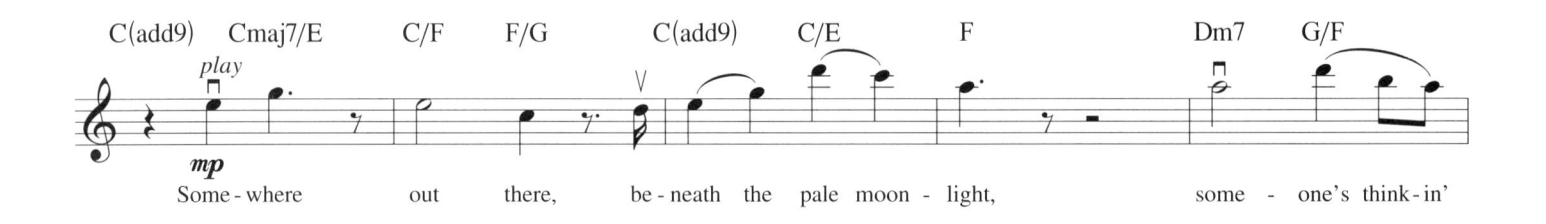

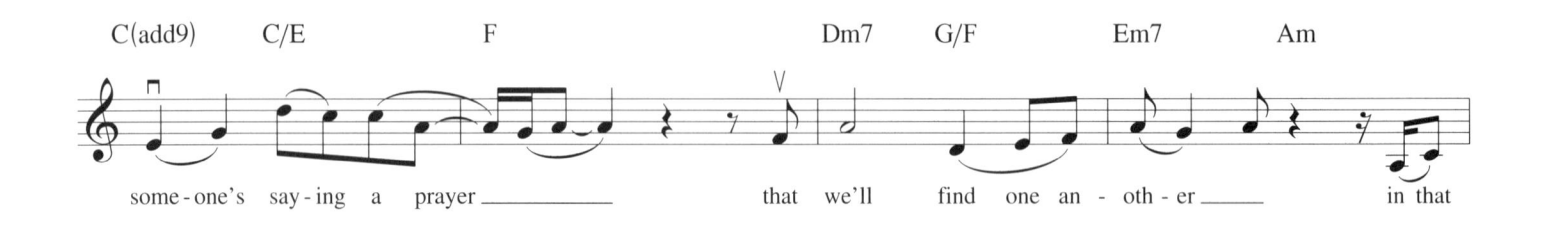

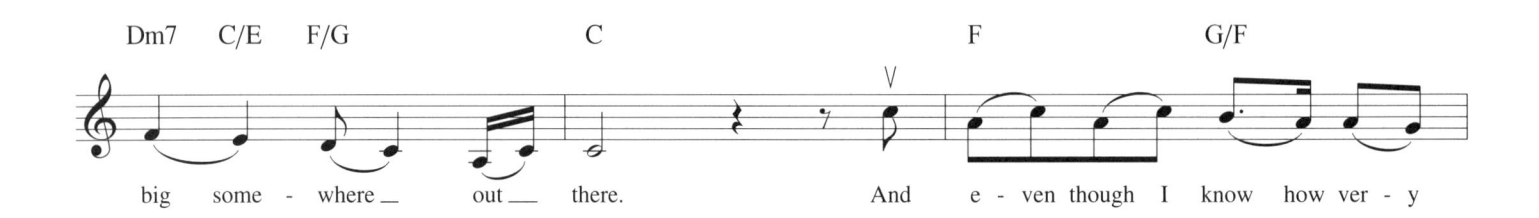

Moderately, with expresson (♩ = 76)

electric piano

Some-where out there, be-neath the pale moon-light, some-one's think-in' of me and lov-ing me to-night. Some-where out there, some-one's say-ing a prayer that we'll find one an-oth-er in that big some-where out there. And e-ven though I know how ver-y

Copyright © 1986 USI A MUSIC PUBLISHING and USI B MUSIC PUBLISHING
All Rights Controlled and Administered by UNIVERSAL MUSIC CORP. and SONGS OF UNIVERSAL, INC.
All Rights Reserved   Used by Permission

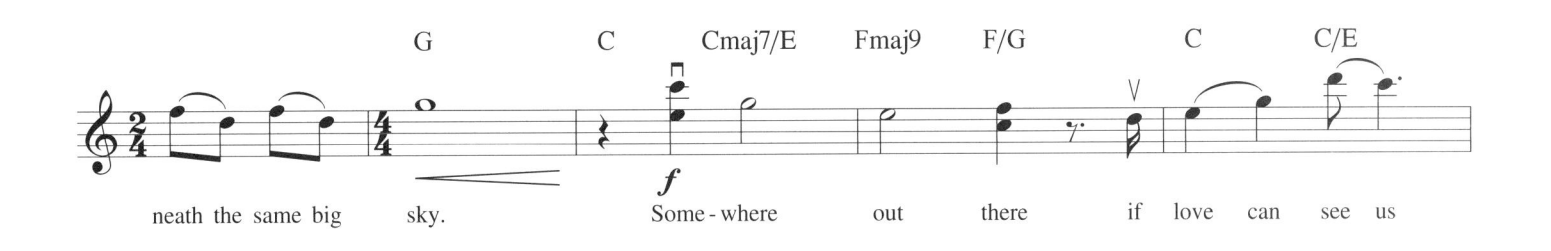

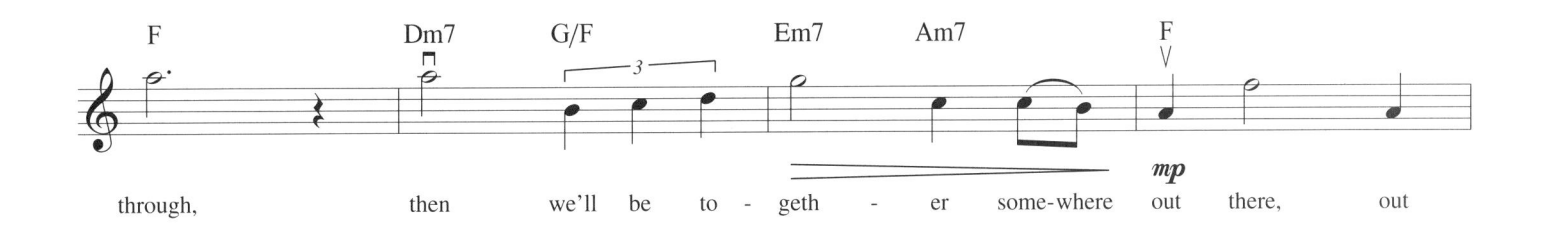

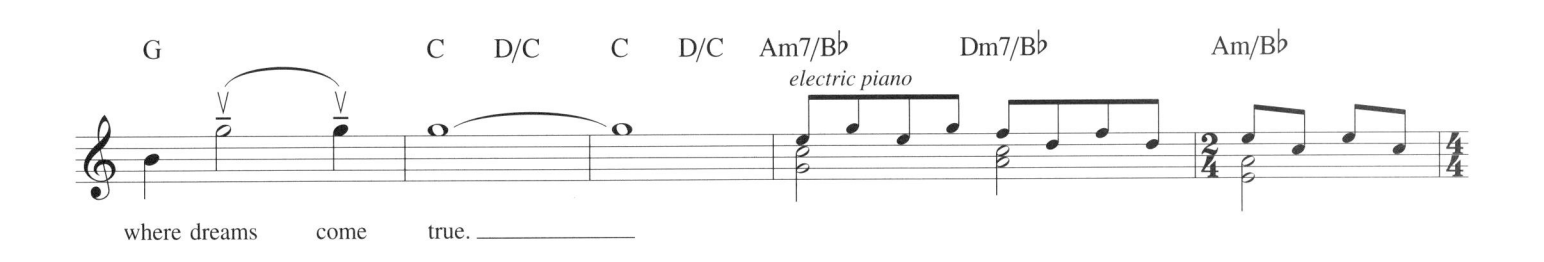

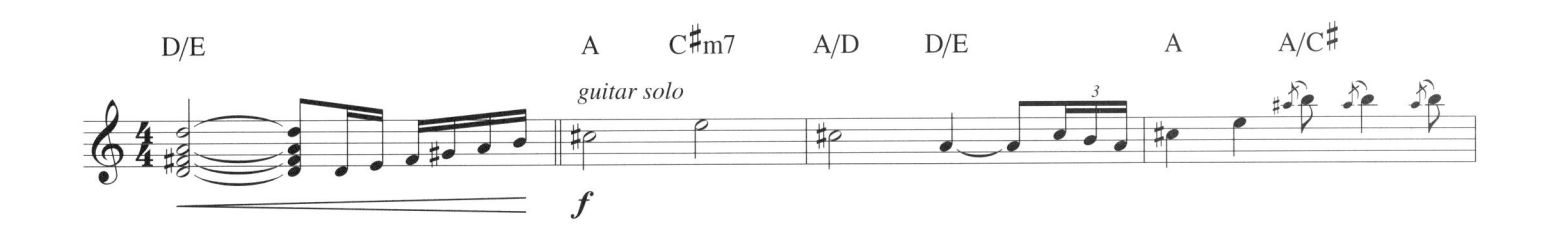

far a-part we are, it helps to think we might be wish-in' on the same bright star. And when the night wind starts to sing a lone-some lull-a-by, it helps to think we're sleep-ing un-der-neath the same big sky. Some-where out there if love can see us through, then we'll be to-geth-er some-where out there, out where dreams come true.

D D+ D6 A/C♯ Bm7 Dmaj7 C♯m F♯m7
Bm7 C♯m D/E A play F G/F
mf
And e - ven though I know how ver - y
F G/F Fmaj7 G/F F G/F
far a - part we are, it helps to think we might be wish - in' on the same bright star. And
A♭ B♭/A♭ A♭ B♭/A♭ A♭ B♭/A♭
when the night wind starts to sing a lone-some lull - a - by, it helps to think we're sleep-ing un - der -
G C Cmaj7/E Fmaj9 F/G C C/E
f
neath the same big sky. Some - where out there if love can see us
F Dm G/F Em7 Am F
mp
through, then we'll be to - geth - er some-where out there, out
G C Cmaj7/E C/F G7sus C(add9)
rit. electric piano
p
where dreams come true.

Highland Cathedral

By MICHAEL KORB and ULRICH ROEVER

Sunrise, Sunset
from the Musical FIDDLER ON THE ROOF

Words by SHELDON HARNICK
Music by JERRY BOCK

Moderately slow Waltz tempo (♩ = 120)

orchestra
mf

play
mf
Is this the lit-tle boy I car-ried? Is this the lit-tle girl at play?

I don't re-mem-ber grow-ing old - er, when did they?

When did she get to be a beau-ty? When did he grow to be so tall?

molto rit.
Was-n't it yes-ter-day when they were small?

a tempo
Sun-rise, sun-set, sun-rise, sun-set, swift-ly flow the days.

Seed-lings turn o-ver-night to sun-flow'rs, blos-som-ing e-ven as we gaze.

Sun-rise, sun-set, sun-rise, sun-set, swift-ly fly the years;

Copyright © 1964 Jerry Bock Enterprises and Mayerling Productions, Ltd.
Copyright Renewed 1992
All Rights for Mayerling Productions, Ltd. Administered by R&H Music
International Copyright Secured   All Rights Reserved

Cm F7 B♭maj7 B♭6 Am7 D7 Gm
one sea - son fol - low - ing an - oth - er, la - den with hap - pi - ness and tears.
Gm D7 Gm D7 Gm G7
Now is the lit - tle boy a bride - groom, now is the lit - tle girl a bride?
Cm G7 Cm A A7 D7♯5
Un - der the can - o - py I see them, side by side.
Gm D7 Gm D7 Gm G7
Place the gold ring a - round her fin - ger. Share the sweet wine and break the glass.
Cm G7 Cm A7 D D7 D+ D7
molto rit.
Soon the full cir - cle will have come to pass.
Gm D7 Gm D7 Gm D7 Gm G7
a tempo
Sun - rise, sun - set, sun - rise, sun - set, swift - ly flow the days.
Cm F7 B♭maj7 B♭6 Am7 D7 Gm
Seed - lings turn o - ver - night to sun - flow'rs, blos - som - ing e - ven as we gaze.
Gm D7 Gm D7 Gm D7 Gm
mp
Sun - rise, sun - set, sun - rise, sun - set, swift - ly fly the years;
G7 Cm F7 B♭maj7 B♭6 Am7 D7 Gm
rit.
one sea - son fol - low - ing an - oth - er, la - den with hap - pi - ness and tears.

A Time for Us
(Love Theme)
from the Paramount Picture ROMEO AND JULIET
Words by LARRY KUSIK and EDDIE SNYDER
Music by NINO ROTA

Slowly and expressively ($\quarternote = 76$)

piano

mp

A time for us some-day there'll be when chains are torn by cour-age born of a love that's free. A time when dreams so long de-nied can flour-ish as we un-veil the love we now must hide. A time for us at last to see a life worth-while for you and me. And with our love through tears and thorns we will en-dure as we pass sure-ly through ev-'ry storm. A time for us some-day there'll be a new world, a

Copyright © 1968 Sony/ATV Music Publishing LLC
Copyright Renewed
All Rights Administered by Sony/ATV Music Publishing LLC, 8 Music Square West, Nashville, TN 37203
International Copyright Secured   All Rights Reserved

world of shin-ing hope for you and me. A time for us some-day there'll be when chains are torn by cour-age born of a love that's free. A time when dreams so long de-nied can flour-ish as we un-veil the love we now must hide. A time for us at last to see a life worth-while for you and me. And with our love through tears and thorns we will en-dure as we pass sure-ly through ev-'ry storm. A time for us some-day there'll be a new world, a world of shin-ing hope for you and me.

We've Only Just Begun

Words and Music by ROGER NICHOLS and PAUL WILLIAMS

comes ___ we smile. ___ So much of life ___ a-head, ___
we'll find a place ___ where there's room ___ to grow. ___ (And yes, we've just be-gun.) ___
Shar-ing ho-ri-zons that are new to us, ___
watch-ing the signs ___ a-long the way. Talk-ing it o-ver, just the two of us, ___
work-ing to-geth-er day to day, ___ to-geth-er, ___ to-geth-er. ___
And when the eve-ning comes ___ we smile. ___ So much of
life ___ a-head, ___ we'll find a place ___ where there's room ___ to grow. ___
___ And yes, we've just be-gun. ___

Wedding Processional

from THE SOUND OF MUSIC

Lyrics by OSCAR HAMMERSTEIN II
Music by RICHARD RODGERS